KRIENG
CHAREONW

Vision for the Nations

FRONTIER PUBLISHING INTERNATIONAL
in association with
WORD PUBLISHING

Word (UK) Ltd
Milton Keynes, England

WORD AUSTRALIA
Kilsyth, Victoria, Australia

WORD COMMUNICATIONS LTD
Vancouver, B.C., Canada

STRUIK CHRISTIAN BOOKS (PTY) LTD
Maitland, South Africa

CHRISTIAN MARKETING NEW ZEALAND LTD
Havelock North, New Zealand

JENSCO LTD
Hong Kong

JOINT DISTRIBUTORS SINGAPORE –
ALBY COMMERCIAL ENTERPRISES PTE LTD
and
CAMPUS CRUSADE

SALVATION BOOK CENTRE
Malaysia

VISION FOR THE NATIONS

© Kriengsak Chareonwongsak 1992

Published by Frontier Publishing International in association with Word Publishing.

ISBN 0-85009-803-3 (Australia 1-86258-216-5)

Unless otherwise indicated, Scripture quotations are from the New International Version (NIV), © 1973, 1978, 1984 by International Bible Society.
Other Scripture quotations are from the Authorised Version of the Bible (AV).

The quotations in the following studies are all used by permission.

Studies 1,24 from *The Normal Christian Life*, by Watchman Nee, copyright © 1961 Angus Kinnear. Published in Britain by Kingsway Publications, Eastbourne.

Studies 3,4,12,14 from *Knowing God*, by J. I. Packer, © 1975, Hodder & Stoughton Ltd., Mill Road, Sevenoaks, Kent.

Studies 3,9,30 from *Know the Truth*, by Bruce Milne, © 1982 by Bruce Milne. InterVarsity Press, P.O. Box 1400, Downers Grove, IL 60515.

Study 4 from *The Knowledge of the Holy*, by A. W. Tozer, © 1961 STL Productions, Kingstown Broadway, Carlisle.

Studies 5,11 from *The Practice of Godliness*, by Jerry Bridges, © 1983 by Jerry Bridges. NavPress, Colorado Springs, Colorado 80935, USA.

Studies 6,22 from *Improving Your Serve*, by Charles R. Swindoll, © 1981, Hodder & Stoughton Ltd. (USA/Canada Winfried Bluth, D-5630, Remscheid, West Germany.)

Study 7 from *I Believe in The Church*, by David Watson, © 1978, Hodder & Stoughton Ltd. (USA/Canada Edward England Books, Broadway House, The Broadway, Crowborough, East Sussex.)

Study 9 from *Dropping Your Guard*, by Charles R. Swindoll, © 1981, Hodder & Stoughton Ltd. (USA/Canada © 1981 Word Incorporated, Dallas, Texas.)

Study 14 from *Signs of the Times*, by Paul Lee Tan, © Assurance Publishers, USA.

Study 15 from *Up to Date*, by Steve Turner, © Hodder & Stoughton Ltd. (USA Lion Publishing, Littlemore, Oxford.)

Study 17 from *The Pursuit of Holiness*, by Jerry Bridges, © 1978 Navpress.

Study 19 from *Jesus Commands Us to Go*, by Keith Green, © Word Books, 9 Holdom Avenue, Bletchley, Milton Keynes, MK1 1QR.

Study 20 from *Destined for the Throne*, by Paul Billheimer, © 1975, The Christian Literature Crusade, Fort Washington, PA 19034.

Study 21 from *The Life of Robert Murray M'Cheyne*, by Andrew Bonar, © reprinted 1972, The Banner of Truth Trust, 3 Murrayfield Road, Edinburgh.

Study 23 from *Pleasing God*, by R. C. Sproul, © 1988, Scripture Press, Raans Road, Amersham-on-the-Hill, Bucks.

Studies 25,29 from *Presenting Jesus in the Open Air*, by Mike Sprenger, © 1988, Word Books.

Study 26 extract from *Biography of James Hudson Taylor*, by Dr and Mrs Howard Taylor, © 1965, Overseas Missionary Fellowship, The Vine, Sevenoaks, Kent.

Study 27 from *Evangelism and the Sovereignty of God*, by J. I. Packer, © 1961 InterVarsity Christian Fellowship, England. Used by permission of InterVarsity Press.

Study 28 from *The Doctrine of Repentance*, by Thomas Watson, © 1987, The Banner of Truth Trust.

Reproduced, printed and bound in Great Britain by BPCC Hazells Ltd., member of BPCC Ltd.

92 93 94 95 / 10 9 8 7 6 5 4 3 2 1

Making the most of the studies ...

Welcome to the Oasis study on *Vision for the Nations!* This book will help you to understand how God feels about world evangelisation. It will also encourage you to see that you have a significant part to play in reaching the nations for Jesus.

We suggest that you take two days to cover each study and therefore two months to complete the book. You might want to work through the material more quickly, but if you take your time you are likely to benefit more. We recommend that you use the New International Version of the Bible (post-1983 version). The important thing is not that you finish fast, but that you hear from God *en route!* So aim to learn well and steadily build the teaching into your life.

Catch the vision
Jesus' great desire was that 'the world may believe that you [God] have sent me' (John 17:21b). Many of us have restricted spiritual vision. Rightly we rejoice over small local Kingdom successes, but wrongly we become too content with them. God has a vision for the nations and wants us to be gripped by it too.

When Isaiah saw the Lord he was changed. Dr Kriengsak looks at this encounter with God and explains what the prophet discovered. He underlines how important it is to have godly characters and touches on such subjects as humility, service, unity, purity, steadfastness, discipline and courage. He also highlights people's desperate need of a Saviour and reminds us that it's our task to reach them.

The three sections under the main text relate to the teaching material. You may be asked to consider some aspect of evangelism, to answer a question, or to do something practical. The questions and Scripture verses have been designed to build you up and encourage you to reach out to others with the gospel.

Build a storehouse
The Bible says, 'Wise men store up knowledge' (Prov. 10:14), and Jesus underlines this when He calls us to '[bring] good things out of the good stored up in [our] heart' (Luke 6:45).

God wants to encourage and inform you through His Word. That's what the 'Food for thought' section is all about. It gives you the invaluable opportunity of hearing from God direct and of storing up what He says to you. **Please use a separate notebook** particularly for this section. Not only will it help you to crystallise your thoughts, but it will also be of tremendous reference value in the future.

As you study, refuse to let time pressurise you. Pray that God will speak to you personally and expect Him to do so. You may sometimes find that you're so enthralled by what He says to you that you're looking up many Scriptures which are not even suggested!

Finally, may God bless you through this book. Catch a new vision from Him and commit yourself to reach the world in your generation.

My food: God's will

'My food,' said Jesus,
'is to do the will of him
who sent me and to
finish his work'
(John 4:34).

If you suddenly found yourself marooned on a desert island, what would be your chief concern? Would you worry most that there wasn't a TV or a bed, a bicycle or a fire? No. Your greatest preoccupation would be, 'How am I going to survive if there's nothing to eat or drink here?' And you would immediately go out in search of something that looked consumable.

Jesus said, 'My food ... is to do the will of him who sent me and to finish his work.' He was effectively saying, 'If natural food is so vital for sustaining physical life, don't you think that it's equally important for you to find the food that keeps you going spiritually?' Sadly, we are often so inclined to the physical that we steadily, and often unconsciously, starve ourselves of the spiritual food that we need to keep us functioning effectively for God.

Nicodemus was locked into the physical. When Jesus started talking about being 'born again' (John 3:3), Nicodemus tried to put a literal interpretation on His words. 'How can a man go back into his mother's womb?' he questioned. The woman of Samaria did the same sort of thing. On hearing Jesus' words about 'living water' (John 4:10), she mistakenly

▓ To consider

We need food and water to live. We also need spiritual food for our well-being. In what ways are you consuming spiritual food?

_____

_____

Be honest, was doing the will of God on your list? YES/NO

▓ To meditate on

God wants you to do His will.
'I desire to do your will, O my God; your law is within my heart' (Ps. 40:8).
'Not everyone who says to me, "Lord, Lord," will enter the kingdom of heaven but only he who does the will of my Father who is in heaven' (Matt. 7:21).
'Then you will be able to test and approve what God's will is — his good, pleasing and perfect will' (Rom.12:2b).

said. 'We've been here thirty years, we've seen only three people saved and we're struggling to keep those.' I ignored their comments. 'God wants to do something powerful in this nation,' I thought. 'All things are possible with Him and I'm going to believe for breakthrough.'

The Hope of Bangkok Church now has about 6,000 members and over 100 daughter churches. We've started our own Bible College too. The people are catching the vision — to reach the world for Jesus. They know that by the year 2000 I want to see churches planted in all 685 districts of Thailand and they're responding. They realise that they're not here just to survive or to enjoy themselves, but to fulfil a great commission — a responsibility that they take very seriously. Hundreds are leaving well-paid jobs, training for ministry and going out with the gospel. God is doing marvellous things through them.

It takes courage to have vision. God doesn't want jellyfish Christians who have no backbone and flop around life. He's looking for people who have caught His vision and who, in their own unique way, are running with it. That's the challenge. It's time to rise to it.

> ➤ Read through the story of Abraham. (Gen. 12—25; Heb.11: 8–12)
>
> ➤ What was his vision? How did it affect his life?

▓ To encourage

If you do not have a vision, don't feel condemned. Vision comes from God, you cannot work it up. God has promised to reveal Himself to His people. 'Come near to God and he will come near to you ... Humble yourselves before the Lord, and he will lift you up' (James 4:8a,10).

God is the utmost. I'm not just here to survive, to enjoy myself. I want to do something and my mission is to do what God wants me to do.
Kriengsak Chareonwongsak

In the year that Uzziah died

B elievers long to receive vision for ministry.
Over the next few days we're going to look
at Isaiah 6 and discover how we can find that
new vision.

Uzziah was a very great and capable king
who governed the nation of Israel almost as
successfully as David and Solomon. Under
him, the Jews enjoyed a time of tremendous
prosperity, peace and stability. Then, after a
fifty-two-year reign, he died. It must have been
very hard for the people to adjust to this tragic
event. While Uzziah was alive, they were
doubtless relying heavily on his human
leadership skills to give the nation its security.
But now that he was no longer there, what
would happen to them?

Isaiah grew up during the reign of Uzziah. He
was a young prophet who may have lived in a
palace and who probably also put his trust in
man's abilities. When Uzziah died, God used
this critical moment to turn Isaiah's eyes away
from man to Himself. Doubtless, Isaiah had
experienced God's touch before. But that day
he was given a vision that would form the
foundation of his ministry for the rest of his
life.

▓ To consider

Is your view of God limited to what you
think He is like or do you have a biblical
view?

Do you simply know *about* God or do
you *know* God?

▓ To meditate on

The Lord wants to meet with you.
'Seek the Lord while he may be found;
call on him while he is near' (Isa. 55:6).
'Break up your unploughed ground; for
it is time to seek the Lord' (Hos. 10:12b).
'He rewards those who earnestly seek
him' (Heb. 11:6b).

God sometimes chooses a major crisis time to bring us into a new relationship with Him. There we are, having a normal week, attending worship meetings on Sundays and enjoying the company of our families or friends when suddenly God breaks in. Up to that point we thought we were doing OK. Now we see God as He really is and the experience has a profound effect on us.

Vision for ministry emerges from a new understanding of God. We so often restrict Him to our rational ways of thinking and almost dictate to Him what He can and can't do. But when He comes to us in a new way, our human logic crumbles — Uzziah dies — and God appears in all His glory. When our eyes are fixed on Him, we find that we're no longer allowing people to dictate to us what will and won't work. And as we experience more of God, He enlarges our vision, increases our faith and enables us to do amazing things that we had never dreamed of doing before.

Isaiah saw the Lord and he was changed. Imagine the impact on the nations if every Christian had a fresh encounter with God and believed Him for mighty breakthrough.

➤ In a notebook make a list of the attributes of God.

➤ Spend time meditating on these qualities and asking God to reveal Himself to you as He really is.

▒ To read

He who often thinks of God, will have a larger mind than the man who simply plods around this narrow globe ... The most excellent study for expanding the soul, is the science of Christ, and Him crucified, and the knowledge of the Godhead in the glorious Trinity. Nothing will so enlarge the intellect, nothing so magnify the whole soul of man, as a devout, earnest, continued investigation of the great subject of the Deity. *C. H. Spurgeon*

Glory is a familiar biblical term, normally conveying the visible manifestation of God's being. His glory carries us to the heart of all that is essential to his being as God, his divine majesty, his sheer *God* ness ... This divine glory is focused only as we fall before him in awe and adoration. *Bruce Milne*

I saw the Lord

I saw the Lord seated on a throne (Isa. 6:1b).

When Isaiah had his vision of heaven, he didn't see some angels in the process of making a throne. The throne was there. And he didn't see the Lord under or beside the throne but seated on it — high and exalted, totally in command, sovereign over everything.

Sometimes we know that God is majestically seated on His throne but act as though He isn't. With one breath we say, 'Nothing is too hard for the Lord' and then we look around at our circumstances and add '... except this'. When we are challenged to have more faith, we try to force ourselves to believe God more. But that doesn't work. Our faith doesn't increase with effort but with revelation. The level of our faith is directly proportionate to the way that we see God.

Just as Isaiah saw the Lord, so individuals whose hearts are open to God are receiving a new revelation of Him. One of them is a lady in her fifties who was converted in one of our churches in the north-eastern part of Thailand. She believes that God is all-powerful and is confident that He will use her. So wherever she goes she lays hands on people and sees wonderful things happen.

▓ To consider

Are there circumstances in your life which make it hard for you to believe that God is sovereign?
What are they?

_____

_____

Ask God to reveal Himself to you, and, give you faith to see these circumstances from His perspective.

▓ To meditate on

The Lord is Sovereign.
'The Lord has established his throne in heaven, and his kingdom rules over all' (Ps. 103:19).
'This is what the Lord says: "Heaven is my throne, and the earth is my footstool"' (Isa. 66:1).
'For nothing is impossible with God' (Luke 1:37).

We held a crusade in one of our daughter churches and God worked miracles. Three people who had been in wheelchairs for two, five and ten years got up and walked. The members of that church have no choice but to believe in the supernatural. It goes on all around them.

Right now the Christians in Thailand are dividing up a map of the world. Some of them are learning Spanish, others Japanese or some other language. Why? Because they've seen a vision of God. For the first time in the history of Thailand, people are preparing to reach the world for Jesus. They're not being compelled, they're being motivated by the desire to do His will. For them, it's a privilege.

I have a great vision for the nations because I've seen a great vision of God. If I look at myself, I'm tempted to think, 'He can't possibly use me.' But then I fix my gaze on His glory and I know that He can do great things through my life. If God is sovereign, then nothing can thwart His purposes. At His word governments rise and fall, storms are stilled and the sick are healed. He is a mighty conqueror and He wants to lead His army to victory.

➤ In a notebook draw a line down the middle of a page; on one side write down human limitations, on the other write down God's corresponding abilities, e.g. we know very little, God is omniscient — He knows everything.

➤ Meditate on the differences between man's abilities and God's.

➤ Spend time worshipping Him, focusing particularly on what He is like, and let faith rise within you as God reveals Himself to you.

▓ To read

Today, vast stress is laid on the thought that God is *personal*, but this truth is so stated as to leave the impression that God is a person of the same sort as we are — weak, inadequate, ineffective, a little pathetic. But this is not the God of the Bible! Our personal life is a finite thing; it is limited in every direction, in space, in time, in knowledge, in power. But God is not so limited. He is eternal, infinite, and almighty. He has us in His hands: but we never have Him in ours. Like us He is personal, but unlike us He is *great. J. I. Packer*

The God we must learn to know is the Majesty in the heavens, God the Father Almighty, Maker of heaven and earth, the only wise God our Saviour. *A. W. Tozer*

Reverence and humility

Above him were seraphs, each with six wings: With two wings they covered their faces, with two they covered their feet (Isa. 6:2a).

The seraphs above the throne were ministering to the Lord in worship. Isaiah watched them and was profoundly affected by their service. Whenever we see others honouring God, we are deeply challenged.

On one occasion I was preaching at a celebration meeting in Thailand. When I'd finished, I invited believers to come forward if they were willing to go anywhere for God. Hundreds of people streamed to the front, knelt down and surrendered their lives to do His will — whatever it was. I wept when I saw their devotion.

The seraphs worshipped God with reverence: they used their wings to cover their faces. In the ancient east, whenever a king or an emperor passed by, the people revered him so much that they dared not look up. Instead, they covered their faces, bowed low and waited until he had gone by before they lifted their heads. They felt that they were not worthy of his majesty.

Although God invites us to approach His throne with freedom and confidence, we must remember that He is a great King above all so-called gods. Those who live close to Him are not

▓ To analyse

Examine your motivation: are you living to please God or to please yourself?

Are you involved in any 'ministry' which glorifies you and not God?

What criteria do you use for deciding to serve? Is it 'I'll do what's convenient for me' or 'is this an opportunity to serve the Lord?'?

▓ To meditate on

The Lord wants us to be humble.
'For everyone who exalts himself will be humbled, and he who humbles himself will be exalted' (Luke 14:11).
'And being found in appearance as a man, he humbled himself and became obedient to death — even death on a cross!' (Phil. 2:8)
'His divine power has given us everything we need for life and godliness through our knowledge of him who called us by his own glory and goodness' (2 Pet. 1:3).

flippant in His presence. They worship Him with holy fear and serve Him with love and integrity.

Another characteristic of the seraphs was that they covered their feet. In other words, they were humble before the Lord. In Thailand, if you point to something with your foot, you will offend people. Feet are considered lowly things. You don't expose them; you hide them. The seraphs were not proud of themselves, they were serving with humility.

'Man looks at the outward appearance, but the LORD looks at the heart' (1 Sam. 16:7b). Like the prophet, Samuel, we can so often be impressed by externals. We see a gifted individual and assume that God will use him mightily. That may be true. But if his attitude is proud — if he's relying on his gifts, then God will humble him. Then He will notice someone unexpected — some David who is faithfully serving Him in obscurity — and He will raise up that individual to a position of honour.

Speaking of Jesus, John the Baptist said, 'He must become greater; I must become less' (John 3:30). That's the attitude that we must adopt. All the glory must go to Him.

➢ Look up Philippians 2:5–11. This passage tells us that our attitude should be the same as that of Christ Jesus.

➢ Consider all that Jesus laid aside to come to earth as a man. Then by comparison think about His lowly upbringing and way of life.

➢ Try to write in a notebook a description of humility based on Jesus' example.

➢ Think of ways in which this should affect your life.

▩ To pray

Ask God to challenge you deeply as you see others serving Him. Ask the Lord to use you.

Ask Him to reveal Himself to you more so that you can serve Him with love, fear and integrity.

When a believer is truly humble before God and his word, he will also be humble about his own gifts, abilities and attainments. He will realize and gratefully acknowledge that all that he is and all that he has comes from the hand of God.
Jerry Bridges

Time for action

With two wings ... they were flying (Isa. 6:2b).

E ach of the seraphs had six wings. Four of these were employed to cover their faces and feet and the other two were used in flying. The emphasis rested on 'being' — they were reverent and humble, and then on 'doing' — they acted.

Who we are is more important than what we do because we minister from what is within. Jesus said, 'The good man brings good things out of the good stored up in him' (Matt. 12:35a). When He appointed the twelve apostles His first concern was 'that they might be with him' and then 'that he might send them out to preach and to have authority to drive out demons' (Mark 3:14b,15). The more Christlike our characters are, the better we will serve Him. What we are is the launching pad for what we do.

Some believers try to reverse the priority. 'Let's get out there with the gospel,' they cry. 'That's our calling! Action everyone!' The zeal is superb but not the character behind it. People who are careless about their personal relationship with God will have limited success because they simply don't have the lifestyle to back up their message.

▓ To consider

Are you involved in serving the Lord already? YES/NO

If not, consider volunteering your help in the church, e.g. stewarding, visiting, crèche, etc.

▓ To meditate on

The importance of serving.
'Whoever serves me must follow me ... My Father will honour the one who serves me' (John 12:26).
'Whoever wants to become great among you must be your servant ... the Son of Man did not come to be served, but to serve' (Matt. 20:26b, 28a).
'Each one should use whatever gift he has received to serve others, faithfully administering God's grace' (1 Pet. 4:10).

If some believers are almost all action, others are nearly all contemplation. 'We must spend large amounts of time in prayer and sorting ourselves out before God will use us,' they say. Certainly spiritual disciplines and holiness are vital for growth, but we mustn't think that we've got to wait until we're perfect before we minister to people.

When the apostle Paul planted churches he was dealing with brand-new converts, but after only a few years, leaders were emerging from among them. They were going on with God and He was giving them positions of responsibility.

The vast majority of believers in Thailand are new Christians. We don't tell them, 'You've got to wait before God can use you.' We know that if we restrict them, they won't develop as quickly as they should. So we let them do things. It's thrilling to see the outcome: believers who are six or seven years old in the Lord involved in local church leadership.

God wants to use you. Don't sit around envying others. Let them provoke you into action. Start serving — even in small things. As you do, God will gradually unfold to you more of His plan for your life.

▨ To pray

Begin to talk to God about what you would like to do for Him. Tell Him about your hopes and dreams. Make a note of them.

Ask Him to reveal to you the things you can do for Him now and how to start.

➢ Look up the word 'serve' using a concordance.

➢ In a notebook list the different ways in which we can serve God.

'Paul, a bond-slave ... ' The more I pondered those words, the deeper they penetrated. This man, the one who certainly could have expected preferential treatment or demanded a high-and-mighty role of authority over others, referred to himself most often as a 'servant' of God. Amazing. He was indeed an apostle, but he conducted himself, he carried himself, as a servant. I found this extremely appealing.
Charles Swindoll

Unity of faith

Τhe word *Thai* means free. Thai people tend to think that freedom is the same thing as independence, so they prefer to do things on their own. This means that when we go in for competitions we often win when we're competing as individuals, but lose when we're working as a team.

Footballers know that they will lose games if they act as individuals — if they hog the ball and try to steal the applause for themselves. That's why they train not only on their own but also as a team. Some Christians haven't learnt this yet. They don't think that they need anyone to help them. But they do. That's why the church is likened to a body. Each part is dependent upon the others. We must discover how to work together because only then will the church grow.

When Isaiah saw the vision of God, he noticed that the seraphs weren't acting independently or preventing the others from serving. They were functioning together, calling to one another about the Lord, ministering harmony. If we want to reach the world for Jesus, we must be united. Over the next few days I want to touch on four key aspects of

▓ To consider

Make a list, in a notebook, of ways in which you can serve God together with others.

Think about ways in which your strengths can compliment another's weakness and vice versa.

▓ To meditate on

We are one in Christ.
'Then make my joy complete by being like-minded, having the same love, being one in spirit and purpose. Do nothing out of selfish ambition or vain conceit, but in humility consider others better than yourselves. Each of you should look not only to your own interests, but also to the interests of others' (Phil. 2:2–4).

unity that Jesus wants to see in His church. The first of these is the unity of faith.

Some people think that Christian unity can be humanly organised. 'It's about getting well-meaning individuals together for a common cause,' they say. But that's not true. Believers are bound together by their faith in the Lord Jesus Christ. He unites us when we believe His Word and are born again. Unbelievers don't live by the truth, so we can neither be united with them nor allow their unbiblical practices into the church. This doesn't mean that we live in mutual hostility. On the contrary, we seek to bring them into the oneness that we have in Christ (John 17:20,21).

We grow in our relationship with God and steadily develop in our knowledge of the truth. Because of this, we should never assume that our particular group knows it all. We could be tempted to say to Christians in other circles, 'We've got it right and you haven't.' But that superior attitude doesn't encourage the unity of faith. We're on the same side! Let's be mature and allow others to differ. If they are seeking the truth as we are, then God will reveal it to us all.

➢ Read through 1 Corinthians 12:14–27.

➢ What does this passage say about:

- independence?
- unfavourable comparison with one another?
- your place in the body?

➢ How do you need to respond to this?

▓ To confess

How do you view other brothers and sisters? Do you think more highly of yourself than others?

Confess any wrong attitudes you have towards specific individuals. (You may actually need to ask their forgiveness or make restitution to them in person.)

Christian unity ... was inaugurated on the cross, is given by God, and wrought by the Holy Spirit in the hearts of his people. And history teaches us that when revival comes, the Spirit takes virtually no notice of denominational labels, and, what is more, those who experience revival do not worry about them either.
David Watson

Unity of life

'I have given them the glory that you gave me, that they may be one as we are one' (John 17:22).

W hen Jesus prayed for His disciples to be one with Him and the Father, He used the language of relationship. He didn't just want us to be saved, merely to receive the seed of eternal life. He wanted us to walk closely with Him so that He could express His life through us and draw others to Him. Unity of faith must lead to unity of life. 'Faith without deeds is dead' (James 2:26b).

Once we understand what Jesus did for us on the cross, we express our gratitude to Him by obeying His Word and submitting ourselves to His will. As we do this, God steadily conforms us to the image of His Son. Unbelievers then begin to see a company of godly people whose quality of life they too long to share.

Jesus prayed to the Father, 'I have made you known to them, and will continue to make you known in order that the love you have for me may be in them and that I myself may be in them' (John 17:26). The unity of our life with Christ will be evidenced by our love for God and for others.

God wants to see harmony in His church, people relating together well — overlooking

❋ To question

Look up 1 John 1:7.
What is the key to having fellowship with one another?

_____

_____

What implications does this have for you?

_____

_____

❋ To meditate on

We should love one another.
'Let us love one another, for love comes from God. Everyone who loves has been born of God and knows God. Whoever does not love does not know God, because God is love' (1 John 4:7,8).
'Be completely humble and gentle; be patient, bearing with one another in love. Make every effort to keep the unity of the Spirit through the bond of peace' (Eph. 4:2,3).

offences, refraining from gossip, humbling themselves rather than speaking their mind. Such attitudes don't come naturally. We have to work at them. Jesus could often have lashed out at people who opposed Him, but He didn't. He lived as a servant and His life was motivated entirely by love.

Before we say or do anything, we must check our motives. Are we acting out of love or is there another reason for our proposed course of action? We can deceive ourselves so easily. That's why we need to stay close to Jesus — because the deeper our relationship is with Him, the less likely we are to sin against Him.

God doesn't only want us to love each other, He also wants us to love unbelievers — which means that we must be sensitive to them. Christians who attempt to ram the gospel down the throats of their victims will succeed only in making them sick of the message. But those who approach people with kindness and concern will eventually win a hearing.

Believers mustn't charge around trying to force people into the Kingdom. They must be imitators of Christ — drawing attention to Him by their godly lives.

▒ To consider

'Do not let any unwholesome talk come out of your mouths, but only what is helpful for building others up according to their needs, that it may benefit those who listen' (Eph. 4:29).
What is unwholesome talk?

_____

What kind of talk will build others up?

_____

➤ Sometimes the very people we want to reach behave like enemies towards us.

➤ Jesus taught that we should love our enemies. Look up these Scriptures and write down how we can do this: Prov. 24:17; 25:21,22; Matt. 5:43,44; Luke 6:27–36; Rom. 12:17–21.

_____

_____

_____

_____

Genuine friendship is vital to our emotional health and well-being. Yet included among the multitudes who settle for shallow, worldly counterfeits are numerous Christians who either cannot accept or understand God's call to community, to a shared life.
Larry Tomczak
People of Destiny Magazine,
July/August 1991

Unity of purpose

'May they be brought to complete unity to let the world know that you sent me and have loved them even as you have loved me' (John 17:23b).

Some people think that unity is an end in itself. 'We must be united,' they say — as if unity were all that mattered. But this kind of unity only makes us inward-looking. It doesn't fulfil the purpose of God. For Him, unity has one overriding goal: that the world may believe. If unity doesn't lead people to Jesus, it's useless.

Christians don't exist for themselves. They have no hidden agenda for personal gain. They don't compete with others for the praise of men. They live for the glory of God and their sole desire is to reveal Jesus to the world so that others might also believe in Him. The Great Commission is not addressed to selected individuals. It's for the whole church. We are all called to work together to bring people into the Kingdom.

The apostle Paul was gripped by this vision. He said, 'I consider my life worth nothing to me if only I may finish the race and complete the task the Lord Jesus has given me — the task of testifying to the gospel of God's grace' (Acts 20:24). Paul knew the heart of God for the salvation of the nations and he would never be sidetracked from that great purpose.

▓ To question

Do you consider your life 'worth nothing' unless you share Jesus Christ?

Maybe you feel that you are a million miles away from having this attitude. But you can change, with small steps. Don't be unrealistic and say 'I will be like that from now on.' The way to start is to ask God to help you begin to understand His desire for the salvation of the nations.

▓ To meditate on

Our overriding purpose is to see people saved.
'I have become all things to all men so that by all possible means I might save some. I do all this for the sake of the gospel, that I may share in its blessings' (1 Cor. 9:22b,23).

It's when you consider God's mercy towards you that you begin to reach out to others. Suddenly you realise how much they are unconsciously depending on you to help them.

I'm just so grateful to God that someone shared the gospel with me — while I was at university in Australia. While in Thailand I had never met a Christian, looked at a church building or seen a Bible. But God saved me through a fellow student and now I live to proclaim the name of Jesus and long to see millions coming to Him to be set free from sin.

By the year 2000 there will be at least six billion people in the world. If we won only half of them, we would need to plant about thirty million churches — and we've got about two million so far! A further twenty-eight million churches will all require leaders and where will they come from? The body of Christ.

We are not only members of God's family. We're also His soldiers. Individually we have specific tasks to do; together we're fighting to retrieve ground taken by our enemy, Satan. Today God is clarifying the goal and mobilising His forces to conquer the world for Jesus. He wants you to be involved.

➤ In a notebook write down anything that can become a hindrance to unity with other believers, e.g. fear, envy, doctrinal differences. (You may find it helpful to think about the relationships between the churches/ Christian groups in your own town.)

➤ Next, write down in a notebook the dynamics which make a team work well together, e.g. common purpose.

➤ Compare the two lists and think of ways in which you personally can be more united in purpose with other believers.

▨ To read

What has happened to our unity? This simple plan, so beautifully articulated by Jesus and so wonderfully begun in the first century, has been woefully complicated and confused by man ... Even the restrictive ranks of evangelicalism are divided into more than thirty various groups, all confessing a common faith in the Lord Jesus Christ. Surely the world scratches its head at that ... The unity He desires is one that strengthens and encourages us in our pilgrimage. In fact, when that unity is present we begin to walk in such confidence that there's a definite hint of invincibility in our faith. It's all part of the way God arranged it. *Charles Swindoll*

The unity of the church derives from its being grounded in the one God (Eph. 4:1-6). All who truly belong to the church are one people and hence the true church will be distinguished by its unity. *Bruce Milne*

Unity of destiny

In his great mercy he has given us new birth into a living hope through the resurrection of Jesus Christ from the dead, and into an inheritance that can never perish, spoil or fade — kept in heaven for you (1 Pet.1:3b,4).

J esus prayed, 'I want those you have given me to be with me where I am, and to see my glory' (John 17:24a). The gospel is not earthbound. Certainly we have to live on this planet for now, but there's an eternity waiting for us. Jesus has prepared a place in heaven for everyone who believes in Him. One day we will stand in His presence and see His glory.

Abraham's eyes weren't fixed on the world's temporary pleasures. He was captivated by something much greater. He was looking forward to a 'city with foundations, whose architect and builder is God' (Heb. 11:10). And Moses rejected Egypt's treasures 'because he was looking ahead to his reward' (Heb. 11:26b). These heroes, and many others throughout history, were building something of eternal value. They saw the invisible and lived for it.

Sadly, some Christians are very short-sighted. They live as if this world meant far more to them than eternity. Some of them tend to be more self-centred than others. They build for themselves a cosy nest on earth and engage in an acceptable amount of Christian activity. Outwardly they seem OK; actually they're too content with the present. They've settled for the

▓ To question

How do we fix our eyes on what is unseen rather than what is seen?

_____

_____

_____

Do you need to shift your gaze onto what is unseen?

▓ To meditate on

We have an eternal destiny.
'Set your hearts on things above ... not on earthly things. For you died, and your life is now hidden with Christ in God. When Christ ... appears, then you also will appear with him in glory' (Col. 3:1b–4).
'In my Father's house are many rooms ... I am going there to prepare a place for you ... I will come back and take you to be with me that you also may be where am' (John 14:2–3).

pleasures around them and have little vision for the future.

Others are more keen to build the church. Rightly they see that the gospel must be relevant to today — that it must have social, political, economic, cultural and personal implications. They reach out to the unsaved and see them converted. God moves powerfully in healing. Marriages are mended, the unemployed find jobs and there are miraculous provisions of finance. The church grows and the people are happy. They praise God for everything He's doing, but their eyes are almost exclusively focused on earthly blessings. They forget that they're building for eternity.

We mustn't be so preoccupied with the progress of the church here that we fail to see something far more glorious to come. God blessed Abraham on earth, but he lived for heaven. Paul planted churches but longed for eternity (2 Cor. 5:1–10; Phil. 1:23). We too must share this unity of destiny. There's an eternal weight of glory coming. 'So we fix our eyes not on what is seen, but on what is unseen. For what is seen is temporary, but what is unseen is eternal' (2 Cor. 4:18).

➢ Read the book of Haggai. In what ways were the people fixing their eyes on what is seen?

➢ What was God's promise to them if they gave their attention to building the Lord's house (what was unseen)?

➢ Notice the phrase 'Give careful thought to your ways' in Haggai 1:7b. Ask the Lord to help you give careful thought to your ways and to reveal any adjustments which you need to make.

▒ To encourage

Sometimes difficult circumstances take all our attention. The Bible teaches, however, that we can have a completely different outlook. Instead of being weighed down by difficulties, we can change our perspective by seeing that we have been raised up with Christ in heavenly places.

'God raised us up with Christ and seated us with him in the heavenly realms in Christ Jesus, in order that in the coming ages he might show the incomparable riches of his grace, expressed in his kindness to us in Christ Jesus' (Eph. 2:6,7).

Blessed Assurance, Jesus is mine!
Oh what a foretaste of glory divine!
Heir of salvation, purchase of God;
Born of His Spirit, washed in his blood.
Fanny Crosby
'Blessed Assurance'

Focus on God

Our society delights in exalting gifted people. You see the fans crowding round their particular star, hoping for his autograph. Later, when they see him in action, they get very excited by his performance. He's their hero, the one they'd love to meet and get to know better.

The seraphs of Isaiah 6 weren't captivated by a fellow being — some sort of high-ranking, gifted angel. They were in the presence of an infinitely greater person. They were calling to one another, exalting the holiness and majesty of the Lord. Their words must have had a powerful impact on the prophet because he repeated the phrase *the holy one of Israel* twenty-nine times in his book.

God was the centre of the seraphs' attention. He must be the centre of ours too. In the church it's very easy to adopt worldly attitudes and begin to exalt human beings too highly. God does choose to give great ministries to certain individuals, but if we're not careful we can idolise them. That's dangerous because people make mistakes. Let's not live as adoring fans of godly men and women. Let's raise our sights and reserve our worship exclusively for the Lord.

▓ To recall

When you were first saved, you were probably counselled to invite Jesus to be the Lord of your life. Think back to that time and consider if you have allowed other 'lords' into your life.

What would you say is the main focus of your life, e.g. family, career? Think of ways in which you can ensure that God is at the centre of your attention in each of these areas.

▓ To meditate on

We are to worship God alone. 'You shall have no other gods before me' (Exod. 20:3). 'What, after all, is Apollos? And what is Paul? Only servants, through whom you came to believe — as the Lord has assigned to each his task' (1 Cor. 3:5).

Not only did the seraphs exalt God, they also praised Him for what He had done. 'The whole earth is full of his glory,' they declared. Their words weren't literal, but prophetic. They didn't actually see God's glory filling the earth. They were looking into the future with the eye of faith and confidently proclaiming in the present what they knew would come to pass.

There's some very pessimistic teaching about the church. Some Christians think that the church will go steadily downhill until Jesus comes and rescues it. I happen to believe that He will return for a glorious bride — from 'every nation, tribe, people and language' (Rev. 7:9b). I don't go around saying, 'Let's be realistic. God can't possibly reach everyone. So what's the point of trying?' By faith I agree with the seraphs that the whole earth is full of His glory.

We are imparting this vision to the church in Thailand. We tell our members that Jesus will be glorified in every people group, and they believe it. They know without a doubt that God will do what He has said. Once they're convinced that the goal will be attained, they are motivated to reach out and accomplish it.

▧ To do

Make a list of faith-building Scriptures.

Write them on a card and put them in your wallet/handbag. At odd moments during the day take out the card and read the verses. As you do so pray that the Lord will increase your faith in Him.

➤ In a notebook write down two descriptions, one of someone whose life is God-centred, and one of someone whose life is man-centred. You may refer back to a biography you have read to help you or write descriptions of people you know.

➤ Which of these two descriptions is most like you?

It is sad that many Christians do not have this aura of godliness about them. They may be very talented and personable, or very busy in the Lord's work, or even apparently successful in some avenues of Christian service, and still not be godly. Why? Because they are not devoted to God. They may be devoted to a vision, or to a ministry, or to their own reputation as a Christian, but not to God.

Godliness is more than Christian character: it is Christian character that springs from a devotion to God. But it is also true that devotion to God always results in godly character.
Jerry Bridges

□ STUDY 12   The power and the glory

'To him who sits on the throne and to the Lamb be praise and honour and glory and power for ever and ever!'
(Rev. 5:13b)

Not only did Isaiah see God as He really is and the seraphs serving Him, he also saw the consequences of the seraphs' ministry. 'At the sound of their voices the doorposts and thresholds shook and the temple was filled with smoke' (Isa. 6:4).

When the Israelites came to Mount Sinai, God descended with thunder, lightning, fire and smoke. The mountain trembled violently and the people were terrified (Exod. 19:14–20). When the apostle John received visions of things to come, he saw the temple 'filled with smoke from the glory of God and from his power' (Rev. 15:8a). As the seraphs ministered, they released the power and glory of God.

The same thing happens with us. As we serve God, He visits us with power and releases His glory among us. Sometimes He manifests Himself through great signs and wonders — but not always. Often He moves in a more gentle way. But there's still an impact.

We see leaders with a passion to reach the nations with the gospel. They preach with faith and we are stirred by their zeal and enthusiasm to proclaim the Kingdom. We begin to share Jesus more with unbelievers and the ungodly

▓ To discover

Seize the next opportunity you have for ministry, e.g. offer to pray for someone who is sick, ask God for a word of knowledge or witness to a friend.

Discover the release of power through your own ministry when you seek to serve the Lord with a pure heart.

▓ To meditate on

The glory of the Lord will be seen through us.
'Arise, shine, for your light has come, and the glory of the LORD rises upon you' (Isa. 60:1).
'And we, who with unveiled faces all reflect the Lord's glory, are being transformed into his likeness with ever-increasing glory, which comes from the Lord, who is the Spirit' (2 Cor. 3:18).

foundations on which our town is built begin to shake with the impact of our ministry.

Ordinary Christians provoke us too. We notice someone in the church. There he is, serving faithfully wherever he goes. He doesn't blow a trumpet to announce himself. He just quietly gets on with the job at hand. As we watch, we sense an inner trembling. 'Lord,' we think, 'you're blessing everything he does. I want to be effective too. Use me more. Release your power in my life. I want to have an impact on others and draw them closer to you.'

God wants to descend from heaven and release His glory in the nations. He's looking for servants who will be channels of His power. They won't be people who essentially live for themselves and do a bit of casual witnessing to save face. God's favour rests not on the lazy but on the diligent — those who abandon their selfish ambitions and live only for Him.

Isaiah caught a vision of the holiness and glory of God and was willing to let God use him. God can do mighty things through people who are humbled by His holiness, captivated by His vision and willing to do anything for the glory of His name.

▓ To ponder

Read Habakkuk 2:14.

If the earth is to be filled with the knowledge of the glory of God, how will this be achieved?

How will God use individuals to reflect His glory?

Think of ways in which you are reflecting God's glory.

➤ Using a concordance look up the word 'power'.

➤ From the references given answer the following questions.

- Who has power?
- Who gives power?
- To whom is power given?

➤ In what ways is power seen in the lives of people in the Bible? Write examples in a notebook.

Do you see the glory of God in His wisdom, power, righteousness, truth, and love, supremely disclosed at Calvary, in the making of propitiation for our sins? The Bible does; and we venture to add, if you felt the burden and pressure of your own sins at its true weight, so would you. In heaven, where these things are better understood, angels and men unite to praise 'the Lamb that was slain.'
J. I. Packer

❏ STUDY 13

He was changed

Since we have these promises, dear friends, let us purify ourselves from everything that contaminates body and spirit, perfecting holiness out of reverence for God (2 Cor. 7:1).

I saiah received vision for ministry. It must have been the most important day of his life. He would never be able to forget that encounter with God, nor the impact that it had on him. He was changed.

If God gives us vision from heaven, we won't light-heartedly trot off and start engaging in ministry. We'll be changed. And later, when we're recounting our experience, we won't refer to it in a casual, matter-of-fact way. We'll speak as Isaiah did — with reverence and awe. The hallmark of any true encounter with God is this: we're never the same again.

People who are committed to establishing God's Kingdom must be different from those around them. Gifting is not sufficient for the task. Saul was a gifted king. Before he was crowned, he met with God who changed his heart (1 Sam. 10:9). But he failed to rule effectively because the change didn't take root. He was probably relying too heavily on his experience of God and on his natural abilities. If we follow suit, we will quit long before we finish the work that God has given us to do.

God doesn't just want us to receive from Him a vision for ministry. He wants us to prove the

---

▧ To consider

Write down any areas in your own life where you need help to change.

_____

_____

Spend time talking to the Lord about them and express your willingness for Him to change you.

▧ To meditate on

The Lord will change us.
'Search me, O God, and know my heart; test me and know my anxious thoughts. See if there is any offensive way in me, and lead me in the way everlasting' (Ps. 139:23,24).
'And the God of all grace ... will himself restore you and make you strong, firm and steadfast' (1 Pet. 5:10).

genuineness of every encounter with Him by our ongoing obedience. He's concerned with the inner man. If we don't intend to obey Him in one area, we're not really obeying Him in any area. So change isn't a one-off thing. It's a continual process of conformity to the Word of God.

Some Christians put more emphasis on counselling than they do on the Scriptures. Certainly, counselling is of value, but it can become a rather self-centred activity. Personally, I prefer to listen to the Word because I know that as I respond to it, God's cleansing power will transform my life.

People who are determined to do God's will must walk with God. If they have a weakness in their character and are unwilling to be changed, then in time their ministry will fall flat. When we choose church leaders in Thailand, we don't seek out perfect people. We look for individuals who are not only keen to be used but who are also responding to God. They may think, 'I don't know how God can use me.' But none of us is sufficient for the task. When God calls us, He will give us the grace we need to get the job done.

▓ To encourage

If, on looking at God, you see things in yourself which you are ashamed of, remember this: God's grace towards us is amazing! Look up Romans 5:20b–21.

'But God demonstrates his own love for us in this: While we were still sinners, Christ died for us' (Rom. 5:8).

▓ Food for thought

➢ Read Acts 5:1–11.

➢ Compare Ananias and Sapphira with Isaiah.

➢ What does this passage tell you about

- their motives?
- their relationship with the Lord?
- how they would have looked outwardly?
- God's knowledge of us?

➢ Read through Psalm 139. Let its truth sink into your heart.

➢ You may want to talk to the Lord about things you have 'hidden' in your heart. Be honest with Him and ask for His help.

Purify my heart,
Let it be as gold and
    precious silver.
Purify my heart,
Let me be as gold, pure
    gold.
Refiner's fire,
My heart's one desire is to
    be holy,
Set apart for You Lord.
I choose to be holy,
Set apart for You, My
    Master,
Ready to do Your will.
Brian Doerksen

Woe to me!

'Woe to me!' I cried (Isa. 6:5a).

T he seraphs worshipped the Lord and Isaiah felt 'ruined' in His presence. That's what happens when you really touch God — you're instantly aware of your bankruptcy. Formerly you were very challenged by sermons about sin and books on holiness. But now you see God and you're devastated.

God never overlooks sin, nor does He treat it lightly. He didn't mildly rebuke the inhabitants of Sodom and Gomorrah, nor blink at the lies of Ananias and Sapphira. He destroyed them. In His opinion, sin is deadly. It is a main cause of sickness, and sentences people to hell. Jesus paid the penalty for sin with His life.

Some of us Christians think that we can get away with sin. 'This particular thing isn't affecting anyone,' we say. 'I'm secure in God's salvation. I just happen to have picked up this little habit. God understands how hard it is. He's merciful and will forgive me.' Sadly, we don't realise that there's no such thing as free sin. We may think that we're succeeding in avoiding punishment when God is actually delaying it to give us time to repent. We may think He doesn't notice, but He isn't mocked. We will reap what we sow. And if we

▓ To ponder

Have you ever spoiled a white T-shirt by washing it with a deep colour? The end result is an off-white garment (or worse).

That is what we are like when we allow ourselves to become tainted by sin, even by so-called 'little' sins. There are no grey areas with God. We need to see sin for what it is.

▓ To meditate on

Understand the seriousness of sin.
'Righteousness exalts a nation, but sin is a disgrace to any people' (Prov. 14:34)
'For the wages of sin is death, but the gift of God is eternal life in Christ Jesus our Lord' (Rom. 6:23).
'If we claim to be without sin, we deceive ourselves and the truth is not in us' (1 John 1:8).

persistently refuse to respond, we will eventually wreck our ministry for Him.

Grace and discipline can't be divorced from one another. Grace totally changes our legal standing with God but it doesn't automatically transform our characters. If we want God to complete the work that He's begun, we must co-operate with Him. He will transform us, but we must discipline ourselves to obey whatever He says. The balanced believer doesn't focus so exclusively on free grace that he minimises the seriousness of sin, nor does he become so legalistic that he forgets God's grace.

If we're content just with a ticket to heaven, we're turning Christianity into something substandard. God wants us to be secure in our eternal destiny, but that's not the complete story. We're involved in a love affair with Jesus Christ. One day He will return for His bride, the church. If you were with Him in heaven now, would you be happy to hear your betrothed on earth saying, 'I'll be faithful for 364 days in the year, but you must let me do what I like on the other day'? Of course not! You'd want to return not for a tarnished bride, but for one who was beautiful.

➤ Compare the following stories: Gen. 6; 13:13; 18:16—19:29; Acts 12:21–23; 13:8–12.

➤ Write down how God feels about sin.

_____

_____

_____

➤ Is this how you feel too?

➤ If not, ask God to give you an understanding of how He feels.

▓ To read

God is the Judge of all the earth, and He will do right, vindicating the innocent, if such there be, but punishing (in the Bible phrase, 'visiting their sins upon') law breakers (cf. Gen. 18:25). God is not true to Himself unless He punishes sin. And unless one knows and feels the truth of this fact, that wrongdoers have no natural hope of anything from God but retributive judgement, one can never share the biblical faith in divine grace. *J. I. Packer*

I'm against sin, I will kick it as long as I have a foot. I will fight it as long as I have a fist, I will butt it as long as I have a head, I will bite it as long as I have a tooth and when I'm old and fistless and footless and toothless, I'll gum it until I go home to glory.
Billy Sunday

I am ruined!

'I am ruined! For I am a man of unclean lips, and I live among a people of unclean lips' (Isa. 6:5b).

B efore he saw the Lord, Isaiah probably didn't think of himself as a particularly bad person, but the day he encountered God, he viewed himself in a new way. The same thing happened in the lives of other Bible heroes.

When righteous Job saw God, he declared, 'I despise myself and repent in dust and ashes' (Job 42:6). When Daniel had an angelic visitation, he was 'overcome with anguish'. He was helpless, strengthless and scarcely able to breathe (Dan. 10:16b,17). When Peter saw Jesus perform a miracle, he fell down and said, 'Go away from me, Lord; I am a sinful man' (Luke 5:8b). And when John received a vision of Jesus, he 'fell at his feet as though dead' (Rev. 1:17a). Immediately God revealed Himself to them, they were ruined.

Society tries its very best to make us feel outwardly acceptable, while God is far more interested in our hearts. When we see Him as He is, we will discover who we really are. As we walk with Him, He will strip away the masks that we wear to protect ourselves from acknowledging the truth. And we will find ourselves confessing specific sins that we've never realised were there.

▓ To reflect

If we are more concerned with the sin of other people than with our own sin we are guilty of hypocrisy. Jesus had strong words for hypocrites: 'You are like whitewashed tombs, which look beautiful on the outside but on the inside are full of dead men's bones and everything unclean. In the same way, on the outside you appear to people as righteous but on the inside you are full of hypocrisy and wickedness' (Matt. 23:27b).

▓ To meditate on

We need to acknowledge our own sin. 'Why do you look at the speck of sawdust in your brother's eye and pay no attention to the plank in your own eye? How can you say to your brother, "Let me take the speck out of your eye, when all the time there is a plank in your own eye? You hypocrite, first take the plank out of your own eye, and then you will see clearly to remove the speck from your brother's eye' (Matt. 7:3–5).

Isaiah suddenly recognised that he was 'a man of unclean lips'. As a young Christian I used to puzzle over the way that many believers talked about one another. With their words they would cut everyone else down to size and make themselves appear wonderful by comparison. 'These people are worse than the communists,' I thought. 'Why aren't they obeying the Word which speaks against such conduct?' But I had to be careful to watch my own speech before I judged others for theirs. Isaiah didn't declare, 'Woe to them! They're ruined!' He had to know that he was at fault before he acknowledged that he lived 'among a people of unclean lips'.

Sadly, we often tend to reverse this order. We dull our ears to personal conviction of sin and point the finger at everyone else. We hear a challenging sermon but instead of applying it personally, we listen on behalf of others. 'So and so needs to hear this,' we think. 'I must send him a cassette of the message.' But it's only as we become aware of our shortcomings that we can help others with similar difficulties. Let's be sensitive to our own sin and be slow to judge others for theirs.

➤ Using a concordance look up every time the words 'speech', 'word(s)' or 'tongue' is mentioned in the book of Proverbs.

➤ In a notebook write down the different kinds of speech, e.g. kind, wise, harsh. Also write down the effects or results of such speech.

▓ To resolve

If you are aware that you are someone with 'unclean lips', confess your sin to the Lord now and ask for His forgiveness.

Resolve that from now on you will be someone whose conversation is 'always full of grace, seasoned with salt' (Col. 4:6b).

You can do this by refraining from speaking negatively and actively seeking to encourage and build up those around you.

Tongue

The tongue is where the
mind comes out into
the open.
Lips move so to speak.
The tongue is where the
mind comes out into
the open
Mind what you say.
Steve Turner

Help!

Then one of the seraphs flew to me with a live coal in his hand, which he had taken with tongs from the altar (Isa. 6:6).

I saiah discovered the seriousness of sin and became sensitive to his own shortcomings. But God couldn't use him powerfully until he had been forgiven. His helper was one of the seraphs. As the angelic being approached, Isaiah didn't shout out, 'Go away! I can manage without you. Why don't you mind your own business?' He humbled himself and accepted the help that was offered to him.

Unbelievers are often reluctant to receive support. They like to feel that they can cope and view help from others as a sign of personal weakness. Christians frequently follow suit. We think that with Christ's strength we should be able to triumph over difficulties, so we turn down offers from other believers and attempt to 'go it alone'. We forget that we're members of one body and that we need each other.

God wants us to build friendships and to be mutually accountable. A few years ago I sent a letter to all our pastors. In it I explained that God had been re-emphasising to me the need for us to continue to be open with each other. I also approached a close friend who is a prominent church leader and said, 'I really want to be transparent with

▓ To ask

Are you struggling with something but have been afraid to ask for help or have even refused help?

God has put us into the body of Christ so that we can help one another *and* be helped by one another.

Resolve today to speak to someone in the church whom you respect (perhaps your pastor, or homegroup leader) and ask them for help.

▓ To meditate on

The wisdom of accepting help.
'The way of a fool seems right to him, but a wise man listens to advice' (Prov. 12:15).
'Pride only breeds quarrels, but wisdom is found in those who take advice' (Prov. 13:10).
'Better is open rebuke than hidden love. Wounds from a friend can be trusted, but an enemy multiplies kisses' (Prov. 27:5,6).

you. If you see anything wrong with my life, please would you tell me? I might not like what you say, but confront me all the same. I'm willing to receive help.'

It's important for church leaders to do this; it's just as important for everyone else. We were never meant to be people who hide away and declare, 'I can manage, thank you. Attend to your own affairs. Go and clean your car.' We were created to be supportive. Each of us needs to be open with someone to whom we can say, 'I'm really struggling. Please pray for me.'

In the independent age in which we live it's vital that we have this kind of transparent relationship with other members of the local church. It's relatively easy for the devil to influence Christians who have a one-ranger mentality. They may say, 'I'm trusting only Christ' when they're actually too proud to admit that they need help. Isaiah was humble and responsive to the seraph. Let's cultivate transparency not by waiting for everyone else to open up first, but by humbling ourselves and allowing others to minister to us.

➢ Using a concordance make a list in a notebook of all the types of 'one another verse' (each other) e.g. love one another, be hospitable to one another. You should find about 30 different ways to 'one another'.

➢ Consider how many of these activities you are involved in either as the recipient or as the initiator.

➢ Take up the challenge to care for other members of the body. Start by taking one of these verses and putting it into practice regularly, then move on to the next.

▓ To consider

Are you accountable to anyone?

Do you have a friend with whom you can be open about yourself?

Ask the Lord to help you as you seek to develop these kinds of relationships. You may want to talk to a friend and ask them if they will take on this kind of relationship with you.

None of us can stand on our own. That's why we need to build friendships, with people to whom we're accountable, with whom we relate, to whom we can open our lives and say, 'I need help.' People we can phone and talk to, come to privately and say, 'I really need help.' This is the kind of relationship we really need.
Kriengsak Chareonwongsak

Willing helpers

With it he touched my mouth and said, 'See, this has touched your lips' (Isa. 6:7a).

The way in which Isaiah was delivered from his problem has something to say to us. There are five lessons that we need to learn and we'll be looking at them together.

Firstly, he accepted help from someone who was willing to give it. One of the seraphs heard his cry of despair and reached out to him. Isaiah didn't run away. He responded. If we have a problem, we must turn to people who want to help us. Some Christians don't do this. Instead, they put up their spiritual antennae and send out signals which say, 'This is my difficulty. If you've got it, can we form a club?' They seem to socialise well but gravitate towards sympathisers rather than people who desire to help.

Secondly, we must go to those who are able to help us. The seraph knew that he had the solution to Isaiah's problem. Many willing believers actually may not have the answer to ours. So if we approach someone and say, 'If I share my difficulty with you, will you keep it a secret?', we should not expect an unqualified 'Yes'. We should be happy with the reply, 'Yes — but only if I can help you. If I can't, you must allow me to tell a more mature Christian who

▓ To consider

Which of the following is a true appraisal?

- I haven't really sinned, I've just fallen a little short.
- What I have done is a sin, I have fallen short of God's standard.
- It was only a little slip, I couldn't help it.
- God knows I'm not perfect so He makes allowances for me.
- That's the way I am and I can't change; God made me that way.

▓ To meditate on

We need to confess our sin to God.
'I confess my iniquity; I am troubled by my sin' (Ps. 38:18).
'For I know my transgressions, and my sin is always before me. Against you, you only, have I sinned and done what is evil in your sight' (Ps. 51:3,4a).
'No-one who lives in him keeps on sinning. No-one who continues to sin has either seen him or known him' (1 John 3:6).

▓ Food for thought

really can bring you through your dilemma.' If we want help, we won't mind if it doesn't come from one of our church leaders. We'll be humble enough to receive it from anyone who has the resources.

Thirdly, we must receive the right kind of help. The seraph didn't try to use his own methods to assist Isaiah. He didn't produce a hot jacket potato from the microwave and say, 'Eat this and you'll feel better.' He got a live coal from the altar of God. Many Christians are after unbiblical solutions to their difficulties. They want people to listen more than help. 'I can't overcome in this area,' they explain. 'It's part of me now.'

Sin is deceptive. If we really want to practise it, we will probably create our own theology to hold onto it. But we can't justify what we're doing if the 'live coal' in the Word of God says, 'That's sinful. You mustn't do it.' It's no good our protesting, 'It feels right' because our feelings can be wrong. And we won't do ourselves any favours by approaching those who will sidestep the truth. God wants us to be totally committed not to our standards but to His — however inconvenient that may be.

▓ To analyse

When we make excuses for our sin we not only try to deceive God, we also deceive ourselves.

Have you tried to rationalise past sin or have you confessed it and asked God to forgive you?

Ask God to help you to see sin in your own life for what it really is and ask for His forgiveness. If you need help, ask for it from someone who is able to help.

> ➤ In a notebook write out the Ten Commandments. This will help you begin to understand God's definition of sin.

> ➤ Read Exodus 20:3–17 to check them.

> ➤ Now turn to the Sermon on the Mount (Matt. 5:17–48) for Jesus' commentary on the commandments.

> The crucial question then is, 'How do we destroy the strength and vitality of sin?' If we are to work at this difficult task, we must first have *conviction*. We must be persuaded that a holy life of God's will for every Christian is important. We must believe that the pursuit of holiness is worth the effort and pain required to mortify the misdeeds of the body ... We must be convinced that 'without holiness no one will see the Lord' (Hebrews 12:14).
> *Jerry Bridges*

Pinpointing sin

'Your guilt is taken away and your sin atoned for' (Isa. 6:7b).

L et's look at the last two things that Isaiah did to overcome his difficulty.

Fourthly, he acknowledged exactly what his problem was. The seraph didn't apply the live coal to the prophet's eyes, hands or feet because there was nothing wrong in these areas. Isaiah was sinning with his lips and it was these that the angelic being touched.

Christians love to rename sin. 'You must expect a few slips,' we say. 'Exceeding the speed limit isn't really that bad, and everyone takes home the office paper. That's one of the perks.' So sin becomes no more than 'being imperfect' and that's something that everyone does now and again.

By using different terminology we do all we can to avoid calling sin by its true name. Imagine Isaiah trying to do that in a counselling session with you. 'I'm feeling a bit out of sorts,' he says. 'Can't understand it. Maybe I'm just tired. I've been under a lot of pressure recently. Had a few minor disagreements with some of the temple priests. They were totally wrong and I told them so. Anyway, I can't seem to shake off this headache. Maybe you could pray for me.'

▓ To reflect

Are you someone who 'does all the right things', e.g. pay your tithe, attend housegroup, sing in the choir?

These activities are fine in themselves, but we can sometimes use them as a 'cover' for the things that are not and which we are not prepared to deal with.

▓ To meditate on

The Lord wants our repentance. 'You do not delight in sacrifice, or I would bring it; you do not take pleasure in burnt offerings. The sacrifices of God are a broken spirit; a broken and contrite heart, O God, you will not despise' (Ps. 51;16,17).

If you have a problem with your teeth, you don't go to a chiropodist. Only a dentist can touch you at your point of need. Christians must stop trying to dodge the truth and face up to their real problem. Only then will they find relief from it.

Finally, we must be thorough. Isaiah was guilty until the seraph said, 'Your guilt is taken away and your sin atoned for.' If we focus on symptoms, we will be semi-delivered, not completely set free. Many of the doctors in Thailand do that. They know that they can get more money if their patients keep coming back. So they treat the symptoms and encourage frequent visits for new prescriptions.

God wants us to uproot anything in our lives that doesn't glorify Him. It's no use your trying to hide behind fervent Christian activity if your marriage is in a shambles or if you're dabbling in even 'small sin'. Both the big and the small roots of sin must come out or they will grow again and imprison you in guilt. So if you're engaging in sin, face up to it and ruthlessly deal with it. If you don't, not only will you jeopardise your ministry, you'll also be ashamed before God at the last day.

➤ Read Matthew 5: 27–29. What is the symptom of this sin? What is the root of the sin?

➤ In a notebook make a list of specific sins, e.g. stealing, murder, gossip, etc. and note down what are the roots of such sin.

▓ To review

Look back over Studies 14–18.

Think about what God has been saying to you about sin. Is there anything you have put off dealing with that came out of these studies?

Do not move on to further studies until you have begun to deal with the issues which have been raised.

You can't be a gardener just by loving flowers. You have to hate weeds. You can't be God's people by purely loving Him. You must also hate sin. That's God's way.
Kriengsak Chareonwongsak

Whom shall I send?

Then I heard the voice of the LORD saying, 'Whom shall I send?'
(Isa. 6:8a)

And now, O Israel, what does the LORD your God ask of you but to ... serve the LORD your God with all your heart and with all your soul?
(Deut. 10:12)

I mmediately Isaiah was set free from his sin, we have the word, 'Then ... ' It's only as we surrender ourselves completely to God that He can use us. Over the next few days we'll be seeing how we can serve Him more effectively.

God's will is that we serve Him. We know that because the question, 'Whom shall I send?' was not on the lips either of the seraphs or Isaiah. In other words, the request wasn't humanly or angelically inspired. It originated with God. The question reveals His heart. He's looking for people who want to fulfil His purpose for their lives.

Not every Christian is willing to be used by Him. Some are content merely to spectate. They watch everyone else and criticise from the sidelines. Others are too busy with their own affairs to discover what God really wants them to do. If we're in either category, it's time to come out! God wants every one of us involved in ministry.

You are a unique individual. No one who has ever been born can replace you. God decided that He wanted you on earth and He has always had a plan for you. Before you even knew Him, He was working in your life,

▓ To assess

List any gifts and talents you have. If you find this difficult, ask a friend to help you assess yourself.

Think of ways in which you can begin to serve using these gifts and talents.

▓ To meditate on

We should serve the Lord in whatever way we can.
'We have different gifts ... If a man's gift ... is serving, let him serve; if it is teaching, let him teach; if it is encouraging, let him encourage; if it is contributing to the needs of others, let him give generously; if it is leadership, let him govern diligently; if it is showing mercy, let him do it cheerfully' (Rom. 12:6–8).

allowing you to go through many different experiences that would shape your character. When you were born again, He commissioned you to serve Him and gave you the opportunity to use your personality, gifts, time, energy, finance — even old age — for His glory.

The problem is that many Christians are zealous when they first believe and then cool off later. 'In a few years' time you'll become mature and settle down,' they tell the new converts who are all bouncy and enthusiastic about Jesus. Although older people will naturally not be as active as those twenty years their juniors, they should never lose their spiritual fervour. There's no retirement in the Kingdom of God. You don't get pensioned off when you reach a certain age! God calls to every generation, 'Whom shall I send?'

You have a special part in the jigsaw and God wants you to find out what it is. Don't squander your life. Pray for God's guidance and get involved — even in small things. Put out the chairs, help in the Sunday School, visit the older church members. Do something! God looks for people who are faithful behind scenes and often leads them into powerful ministries.

➢ Read through the book of Jonah. Jonah was a man who knew it was God's will for him to preach to the people of Nineveh.

➢ In a notebook write down:

- What were the consequences of Jonah's disobedience?
- What were the consequences of Jonah's obedience?
- What would have happened to the people of Nineveh if Jonah had not finally obeyed God?

➢ Can you think of any examples in your own life where you have not obeyed God's expressed will for you? If it is not too late why not put it right now?

⬛ To ponder

Think about what it means to 'serve the Lord your God with *all* your heart and *all* your soul'.

Write a list of what *all* means to you in this context, i.e. all my energy, all my finances.

**Jesus commands us to go,
It should be the exception
if we stay.
It's no wonder we're
moving so slow,
When His church refuse to
obey,
feeling so called to stay**
Keith Green

And who will go for us?

'And who will go for us?' (Isa. 6:8b)

I t makes a lot of difference how Christians see themselves. If you think you're a mere slave who's being forced to obey God's orders, you'll either withdraw into servitude or rebel and clear off. But if you realise that you're responding to God's call to 'go for us', you will be filled with a great confidence. 'God has commissioned me to be His ambassador,' you will declare. 'He's given me His authority — so I can be bold for Him.'

Only disobedient believers need be discouraged. Those who are running in God's purposes should know that all heaven is behind them. 'I'm not serving in my own strength,' they will say. 'I'm acting as God's representative, doing things that He would do if He were physically present on this planet. I'm here in the name of the Lord of Hosts. He and the angels are on my side and Satan and his demons tremble even at the thought of Christ's power in me.'

Jesus has given us authority to take ground for Him. If you believe this and go out on His behalf, God will vindicate you. I once stopped my car in a city in Thailand where there wasn't one single church. I got out, laid my hand on

▓ To do

Look up the word 'ambassador' in a dictionary.

What similarities are there between the way we serve the Lord and the way in which an ambassador serves a king or government?

▓ To meditate on

We have been given authority.
'I will give you the keys of the kingdom c heaven; whatever you bind on earth wi be bound in heaven, and whatever you loose on earth will be loosed in heaven' (Matt. 16:19).
'Go and make disciples of all nations, baptising them in the name of the Fathe and of the Son and of the Holy Spirit ... And surely I am with you always, to the very end of the age' (Matt. 28:19,20b).

the ground and said, 'In Jesus' name I'm claiming this town for the Lord.' Eventually, I had the joy of seeing that city and many others open up to the gospel.

I'm looking forward to the day when Thai believers will be working in all the countries in the world. I think about Moslem lands where it's desperately hard to witness for Christ. But I don't despair. If God can penetrate godless Thailand, then He can break into the greatest strongholds of the enemy as well. Nothing is too hard for the Lord.

God wants us to go for Him, to conquer territory in His name by establishing churches throughout the world. Sometimes it will be a fierce battle but God promises us His resources to overcome. The victory already belongs to Him, so we don't need to be afraid of the task that He gives us to do.

Isaiah's eyes had 'seen the King, the Lord Almighty'. The prophet knew the One who would support him if he accepted the commission to be His representative on earth. We see God with the eyes of faith. If we believe in His authority, He'll release His power through us. Exciting idea?

➤ Begin a study in the book of Acts, noting down in a notebook every time someone served on the Lord's behalf and the authority given to them, e.g. authority to heal, to preach, etc.

▓ To encourage

Have you previously disqualified yourself from serving the Lord because of your own weakness or lack of power?

Here is good news for you! *You* have God's authority and power when you are serving on His behalf.

'As the Father hath sent me, even so send I you' can mean nothing less than that we are His deputies with full authority to enforce the divine will and program. The deputy is invested with the full power of the office of his Chief, and is fully authorized to act in His stead.
Paul Billheimer

Here I am! Send me!

God delights to see people volunteer themselves for work in the Kingdom. If we remain deaf to His call, He may discipline and still use us (like Jonah), or find someone else to replace us (as David replaced Saul). Throughout history there have been many Jonahs and Sauls — great disappointments to God. But there have also been the Isaiahs who have responded with willing hearts and who have completed the work that God gave them to do.

When Paul was converted on the road to Damascus, he didn't say, 'Right, Jesus. You know I'm a very capable man. This is what I'm going to do with my life.' He said. 'What shall I do, Lord?' (Acts 22:10a). Paul was releasing both his desires and his abilities into the hands of God. He was volunteering himself to do the Father's will. God is looking for people who willingly give themselves to Him.

I'm amazed at the way He works in the church. From a human point of view, many believers have very little gifting. We might glance at them and think, 'He's very ordinary. I don't expect he'll do much for the Kingdom,' or, 'She's got no real skills. I dare say God will give

▓ To consider

Are you involved in any serving that is not out of a willing heart? Have you been coerced into 'volunteering'?

Take stock of any ministry you are involved in. Are you serving willingly? Consider putting down any responsibilities which have become 'dead works' and seek the Lord afresh for new direction, or a change in your own attitude.

▓ To meditate on

God created us to serve Him.
'For it is by grace you have been saved, through faith — and this not from yourselves, it is the gift of God — not by works, so that no-one can boast. For we are God's workmanship, created in Christ Jesus to do good works, which God prepared in advance for us to do' (Eph. 2:8–10).

her some trivial task to do.' Then we find that God cuts right across our expectations and blesses them to the hilt. We scratch our heads and wonder, 'What is it with them?' And the answer is, their hearts are right. They've willingly given themselves to God. They know that they don't have much ability, but they trust Him to help them and work hard. God can't resist exalting that kind of person, and humbling many others who think too highly of themselves.

God looks not for gifting but for willingness. 'Who will go?' He asked, not, 'Who's qualified to go?' He didn't say to Isaiah, 'Now I'd like you to write down your qualifications and job experience and give me details of your present employment. Then you can say in 250 words why you think that I should choose you for this task.' Certainly, He will use whatever gifts we have, but only if we surrender them to Him.

Isaiah didn't have to serve God, he wanted to. He realised that he would never receive a higher calling and longed to embrace it. God won't compel you to serve Him. Love doesn't force, it draws. If you love Him, why not volunteer yourself afresh into His service?

➤ Over the next week or so try to read a Christian biography. Think about the way the person served God.

➤Write down in a notebook a list of their attitudes, e.g. always thankful.

➤ Take note of any struggles which the subject had in connection with volunteering freely.

➤ List particular events/ situations which challenged you.

➤ Where there are characteristics which you aspire to, talk to the Lord about them and ask Him to help you make changes in your own life.

▧ To do

Spend time alone with the Lord. Meditate on His love for you, worship Him.

Open your heart to Him, tell Him just how you feel about Him and how much you want to serve Him.

If I am to go to the heathen to speak of the unsearchable riches of Christ, this one thing must be given me, to be out of the reach of the baneful influence of esteem or contempt. If worldly motives go with me, I shall never convert a soul, and shall lose my own in the labour.
Robert Murray M'Cheyne

I'm giving up

He said, 'Go and tell this people: "Be ever hearing, but never understanding; be ever seeing, but never perceiving." Make the heart of this people calloused; make their ears dull and close their eyes. Otherwise they might see with their eyes, hear with their ears, understand with their hearts, and turn and be healed' (Isa. 6:9,10).

If Isaiah had known what God was going to ask him to do, he might not have been so quick to volunteer himself! But that's the challenge to each one of us. God is delighted when we say, 'Send me!' before we fully understand what He wants us to do. If we are motivated by fear, we will expect to know in advance exactly what we're letting ourselves in for. But if we're motivated by faith and love, we won't mind. Our sole preoccupation will be to do His will — regardless of the cost.

God warned Isaiah that the people would be unresponsive to his message. Then He outlined what the prophet could expect from them. First, they would resist him with their hearts, then with their ears and finally with their eyes. That's the three-stage process of hardening. Your heart condition will dictate how you hear and see. So if you've closed your heart to something, you'll cut yourself off from it. When someone preaches on that particular subject, you'll be deaf to it and blind to what God is trying to show you.

How did God want Isaiah to react to this unresponsive people? Should the prophet give up on them? As they persistently refused his

▓ To consider

Have you ever given up on something because you didn't see any fruit?

In retrospect can you see what God was doing?

▓ To meditate on

Don't be discouraged.
'Not only so, but we also rejoice in our sufferings, because we know that suffering produces perseverance; perseverance, character; and character, hope' (Rom. 5:3,4).
'Thus the saying "One sows and another reaps" is true' (John 4:37).

message, he would certainly be tempted to do that. But God told him that he must keep reaching out to them, whether they turned from their sin or not.

When we earnestly respond to God in a new way, our first thought might be, 'He's bound to bless my efforts. After all, I'm doing His will.' Then reality sets in. We launch out and hit one problem after another. People refuse to respond, they're nasty to us or just plain indifferent to what we have to say. After a few months, we're thinking, 'I'm getting nowhere. What's the point of carrying on?'

If God calls you to do something, He doesn't want you to resign before it's done. There will be encouraging times, but success doesn't come without effort. If you want your ministry to count for God, you must understand that there's a price to pay. You can't get away with a half-hearted response to God's plan for your life. Either you're thoroughly involved in it or you're not. If you say, 'Yes, I'm going to press on regardless,' you will resist the temptation to give up when everything seems unfruitful. Don't give up. Complete the work. In God's time you'll see breakthrough.

➢ Apparent unfruitfulness may seem like real hardship to us. Compare the following passages: 2 Cor. 4:8,9; 2 Cor. 11:23–28; Heb. 11:35–39.

➢ The apostle Paul regarded these as 'light and momentary troubles'.

➢ Read 2 Corinthians 4:16–18. The key for Paul was to fix his eyes on what is unseen. Consider how you can do this.

▓ To assess

is not only those we are going out to who may have hard hearts. We are also susceptible to being deceived by sin and our hearts being hardened towards God.

this the case with you? If so, ask the Lord to reverse the hardening process in you.

Many a Christian, unfortunately, is side-lined today, eaten up by the acid of resentment and bitterness, because he or she was mistreated after doing what was right.
Charles Swindoll

Don't quit

Then I said, 'For how long, O Lord?' And he answered: 'Until the cities lie ruined and without inhabitant, until the houses are left deserted and the fields ruined and ravaged, until the Lord has sent everyone far away and the land is utterly forsaken' (Isa. 6:11,12).

Isaiah was willing to press on through unfruitfulness, but he wanted to know for how long he had to proclaim the message. God didn't hide the truth from His servant. He told him straight that he would have to preach until the land was deserted. In other words, 'Isaiah, you must keep going until there's no one left to hear you. Either they'll repent or your message will drive them away.'

When people persistently refuse to respond, we desperately want to know when the breakthrough will come. 'For how long, O Lord?' we ask with Isaiah. And God's answer is the same for us as it was for him: 'You must minister to the very end. Preach in one town and when no one wants to listen to you any more, move on to the next and do the same. Keep going from country to country and nation to nation until you've reached the whole world for Jesus. That's the vision. You mustn't quit until the job's done.'

While I was in Scandinavia a pastor came up to me and said, 'I'm so pleased you're coming to my church this Sunday because I'm just about to retire.' I replied, 'God forbid! There's no retirement in the Kingdom. You're in God's

▓ To do

Make a list of any tasks or projects which you have left unfinished.

Set yourself some goals for completing these and begin to work through them one by one until they are all finished.

▓ To meditate on

We must carry on until the work is done 'Tell Archippus: "See to it that you complete the work you have received in the Lord"' (Col. 4:17).
'But you, keep your head in all situations, endure hardship, do the work of an evangelist, discharge all the duties of your ministry' (2 Tim. 4:5).
'Let us run with perseverance the race marked out for us' (Heb. 12:1b).

army. He won't let you fossilise in a rocking chair! There's far too much work for you to do. Get on with it!'

Some ministers say to the young people, 'I've done my share of the work. I'm getting a bit old for all this. It's your turn now.' That's the wrong attitude. You can't sit back and declare, 'It's time I stopped' — however antique you may be! Why? Because the job isn't complete. We can't decide, 'I've finished now.' We've only just started! There's a world out there waiting for us. I'm not drawing back. I'm looking ahead. My heart burns to see someone replacing me in my country so that I can move onto another place and plant a church there.

When problems come, it's easy to lose vision. We look around at other Christians and think, 'What's the point of pressing on? Everyone else seems to be focusing more on having a good time than fulfilling a goal. Why should I have to carry God's burden for the world?' It's so tempting to drift into 'laid-back' Christianity. God wants to hear you say not, 'For how long?' but, 'I'm totally committed to your plan, Lord. And I'll keep going until everyone has heard the glorious gospel of Jesus Christ.'

➢ Read through the story of Joseph in Genesis 37 and 39 to 47.

➢ In a notebook list the reasons he could have given for giving up.

➢ What was it that kept him going?

▨ To encourage

We are not on our own when we are serving the Lord. His Word says that He will never leave us or forsake us. He is faithful to us.

Review God's faithfulness to you throughout your Christian life. Spend time meditating on His faithfulness.

Never, never never ... give up.
R. C. Sproul

As gold

'And though a tenth remains in the land, it will again be laid waste. But as the terebinth and oak leave stumps when they are cut down, so the holy seed will be the stump in the land' (Isa. 6:13).

G od told Isaiah that even if a tenth of the people remained, the land would again be laid waste. The only thing of lasting value would be the 'holy seed' which would be 'the stump in the land'. What's this saying to us?

Well, the tenth represents those who respond to the gospel. We should see this not as a literal but as a representative figure. God is simply telling us that those who receive the Word will be in the minority. They are the 'remnant chosen by grace' (Rom. 11:5).

If we are faithful in our service to God, He will bless us. He has decided that His Kingdom will be populated by people from every nation and tongue. This must mean that wherever we go, God has prepared some hearts to respond to Him through our message. If we believe this, we will keep proclaiming the gospel even in the face of tough opposition. We will long to reach those whom God has chosen to be His own.

God says that the remnant will be 'laid waste until the 'holy seed' remains the 'stump in the land'. In other words, Christians will be tested. God will scrutinise our lives and our service for Him. What's important to Him is what's left behind after He has refined us. When He looks

▓ To reflect

Can you think of times in your life when God was testing you? (It may be that you put them down to having a 'rough patch'.)

Write down in a notebook anything which you can now see was refined from your life. Thank God for His dealings with you as an individual, ask Him to help you keep holy and blameless, 'a stump in the land'.

▓ To meditate on

Our lives and work will be tested. 'This third I will bring into the fire; I will refine them like silver and test them like gold' (Zech. 13:9a). 'If any man builds on this foundation using gold, silver, costly stones, wood, hay or straw, his work will be shown for what it is, because the Day will bring it to light. It will be revealed with fire, and the fire will test the quality of each man's work' (1 Cor. 3:12,13).

at you, will He see a self-centred, spineless believer who really doesn't care much about establishing the Kingdom of God? Or will He see someone who is zealous for His glory, someone who is holy and blameless, who will be a stump, a stabilising influence in the land?

Many Christians will be embarrassed when God tests them. Some church leaders have consistently resisted new moves of the Holy Spirit among their people and have taken refuge in professionalism. The focus of many believers is on external conformity, not internal holiness. They want to look good on the outside, but they're hiding numerous sins in their hearts.

Jesus is looking for a radiant bride who will be completely faithful to Him. Day by day He will test your genuineness to find out if He can rely on you to fulfil His purposes. He will strip away the façade and challenge your attitudes and actions to ascertain if they're pure. And He will discover whether you're trying to build something for your own glory or for His. If you respond positively to His discipline, He will bring you forth as gold and bless everything you do for Him.

▓ To pray

Spend time with the Lord, tell Him that you willingly accept His discipline, and ask Him to bring you forth as gold.

➤ Read through the story of Job.

➤ In a notebook write down the different ways in which he was tested. Note how he responded to the tests. What happened to him after the testing? Imagine yourself in Job's shoes; how do you think you would respond?

God must bring us to a point — I cannot tell you how it will be, but He will do it — where, through a deep and dark experience, our natural power is touched and fundamentally weakened, so that we no longer dare trust ourselves. He has to deal with some of us very strangely, and take us through difficult and painful ways, in order to get us there. At length there comes a time when we no longer 'like' to do Christian work — indeed we almost dread to do things in the Lord's Name. But then at last it is that He can begin to use us.
Watchman Nee

Be bold

After John was put in prison, Jesus went into Galilee, proclaiming the good news of God. 'The time has come,' he said. 'The kingdom of God is near. Repent and believe the good news!' (Mark 1:14,15)

While each of us has a specific work to do for God, we are all commissioned to proclaim the good news. At this point I want to leave Isaiah and focus on how we can be effective at sharing our faith with others. Let's look first at Mark 1:14–15.

At the time of Jesus, Galilee was under the Roman Empire and Herod was governor of the area. When John the Baptist came on the scene, he boldly denounced Herod for his unlawful relationship with Herodias and was promptly thrown into prison. He had crossed the authorities and would suffer for it.

If we'd been Jesus, we might have noted John's fate and decided to leave it a month or two before we began our ministry. 'It's best to let the dust settle a bit,' we'd have said. 'There's no point in taking chances.' But Jesus didn't wait. Immediately John was imprisoned, Jesus was preaching. He wasn't dominated by fear. He could face every situation with boldness.

Many believers have confronted the authorities with great courage. When John Bunyan was in prison, he was told, 'We'll let you go if you stop preaching the gospel.' He replied, 'If you release me today, I'll be

▓ To consider

What do you fear that makes you afraid to share the gospel, e.g. fear of losing your reputation?

_____

_____

Are these fears legitimate? YES/NO

▓ To meditate on

We are to be bold.
'The wicked man flees though no-one pursues, but the righteous are as bold as a lion' (Prov. 28:1).
'I am not ashamed of the gospel ... it is the power of God for the salvation of everyone who believes' (Rom. 1:16a).
'For God did not give us a spirit of timidity, but a spirit of power, of love and of self-discipline. So do not be ashamed to testify about our Lord' (2 Tim. 1:7,8a).

preaching by tomorrow so you might as well keep me here.' Some people aren't very happy about our evangelistic activities in Bangkok. They spread rumours hoping to provoke the government to get rid of the church. I've told the people that one day we're going to come up against the enemy in a big way. It doesn't worry them. They just keep sharing the gospel.

The early disciples weren't surprised when they clashed with the authorities. Jesus had warned them that they would be hated for His sake. So they didn't tremble with fear when the opposition came. They prayed that God would help them to speak 'with great boldness' (Acts 4:29b) and He answered their prayer. They were filled afresh with the Holy Spirit and spoke the word of God boldly' (Acts 4:31b).

If you are faithfully living and witnessing for Jesus, you can expect trouble sooner or later. So don't be surprised when it comes, and don't withdraw into fear. The Almighty God is on your side. Pray for boldness and stand up for what you believe to be the truth. Dare to be different from everyone else. You have the words of eternal life. Don't let anything stop you from proclaiming them.

▩ To reflect

At its root, fear is not trusting in God, e.g. fear about finances reveals a lack of trust in God's provision, fear for the future reveals a lack of trust in God's sovereignty, etc.

Go back to your study of the attributes of God (Study 3). Meditate on each one and, as you do so, let trust in God and who He is dispel your fears.

➤ Read Daniel 3:8–30 and Daniel 6.

➤ What was the consequence of the boldness of Shadrach, Meshach, Abednego and Daniel?

➤ How did the Lord vindicate His name?

We are living in exciting times. Christianity is at last being seen as something far more dynamic than 'pew-filling and lending a hand to the needy'. It is a high-quality way of life which encompasses a whole supernatural dimension. Such good news cannot be allowed to lie dormant within us or to remain confined in our fellowship meeting places. We dare not just wait for people to come to us before they ever hear the gospel. The command from Jesus to His followers was not 'sit and wait' but 'go and make' (Matthew 28:19)!
Mike Sprenger

In difficult places

Peter says that Jesus began His ministry 'in Galilee after the baptism that John preached' (Acts 10:37). It would have been easier if Jesus had started His ministry elsewhere. The Jewish people didn't have much sympathy for the Galileans. When Nathaniel heard that Jesus came from Nazareth in Galilee, he said, 'Can anything good come from there?' (John 1:46). If the Jews were resistant to the Galileans, they would doubtless be resistant to Jesus as well.

While I rejoice over the missionary work that's being done in the Philippines, I am concerned at the increasing Christian population of that country. Missionaries can opt to go there because it's easier than it would be elsewhere. But if we stay too long in one place, what will happen to the lands where there are no believers at all? Asia is the least evangelised continent but it comprises 59% of the world's population. A few Christians are there, but God wants to see a lot more joining them.

Jesus didn't run away from Galilee because He knew that the going would be tough there. He started where it was hard. We're so often

▓ To question

In your own sphere of influence list the places which you consider to be difficult.

_____

_____

Have you ever tried to infiltrate them?

Why not take just one of these areas and begin to pray that the Lord will show you how to go into this difficult area?

▓ To meditate on

We must preach the gospel.
'The Spirit of the Sovereign Lord is on me, because the Lord has anointed me to preach good news to the poor. He has sent me to bind up the broken-hearted, to proclaim freedom for the captives and release from darkness for the prisoners' (Isa. 61:1).
'I am compelled to preach. Woe to me if I do not preach the gospel!' (1 Cor. 9:16b)

tempted to avoid difficult areas. With our lips we say, 'Lord, I'll go anywhere for you' but in our hearts we add the condition, '... so long as it's not too difficult'. Sometimes we're after success more than faithfulness. Certainly God wants us to be successful at reaching people, but we mustn't aim for easy success and be unwilling to go where the work will be hard.

We're living in an important day. Life means nothing unless we're involved in establishing the Kingdom. God is calling us to take the gospel not to a few lands but to the ends of the earth. I praise Him for those who have already made great sacrifices and gone out. Now I want to challenge new workers to serve, not where it's cosy, but where it counts.

Peter says that Jesus' ministry started in Galilee which, by implication, means that He moved on from there to other places. He doesn't want the church to get stuck in certain locations, but to reach out into new areas. If God isn't asking you to go abroad, pray for labourers who will go, and be willing to launch out into difficult situations at home yourself. But if God is saying to you, 'I want you to serve me overseas,' pray for His guidance and go.

➤ Paul left Titus behind in Crete to carry on what he himself had begun and to establish the church there. Sounds glamorous doesn't it? But read Paul's description: Titus 1:10–14.

➤ It was in fact a difficult place. Imagine how daunting the prospect could have appeared to Titus.

➤ Think about how you would respond to a commission like this. Where should you look for encouragement?

▨ To consider

What do you measure your success by?

Is it by visible results?

The true measure of success is whether or not we have done the will of God.

The overwhelming greatness of the task before the Mission is felt rather than dwelt upon, for yet another Reality shines out from these pages, pre-occupying mind and heart. Than the greatness of the need, one thing only is greater — the fact of God: His resources, purposes, faithfulness, His commands and promises.
Dr and Mrs Howard Taylor

Preach the good news

After this, Jesus travelled about from one town and village to another, proclaiming the good news of the kingdom of God (Luke 8:1a).

For I resolved to know nothing while I was with you except Jesus Christ and him crucified (1 Cor. 2:2).

For what I received I passed on to you as of first importance: that Christ died for our sins according to the Scriptures, that he was buried, that he was raised on the third day according to the Scriptures (1 Cor. 15:3–4).

One person will state, 'The church is here primarily to develop social welfare. We must help the poor, reach out to drug addicts and prostitutes and build hospitals and schools.' Another will say, 'We must tell unbelievers how Jesus can meet their immediate needs.' A third will declare, 'We don't actually need to say anything about Jesus. We should just let our light shine before men and they'll be impressed and glorify God.' And a fourth will suggest. 'We must seek to understand the beliefs of others.'

Certainly Jesus wants us to be involved in these things, and many others. But if we make any of them our top priority, we will be guilty of proclaiming a man-made gospel. We may succeed in filling church buildings with interested spectators, but we won't populate heaven with believers, or earth with disciples.

What was Jesus' number-one goal? To preach the good news. That's our greatest calling! All our outreach will be meaningless unless we proclaim the central message — that Jesus died for our sins. Loving people won't change them. Encouraging them to add Christ to their lives won't bring them out of darkness

▓ To consider

Have you chosen simply to 'let your light shine' rather than actually to speak to people about Jesus?

In a notebook list your non-Christian contacts and friends. With how many have you shared the gospel? Set a realistic goal to share the gospel with a number of them, e.g. in six months I will share the gospel with two people from my list. Start to pray for opportunities.

▓ To meditate on

We must tell the good news about Jesus 'How, then, can they call on the one they have not believed in? And how can they believe in the one of whom they have not heard? And how can they hear without someone preaching to them?' (Rom. 10:14)
'But even if we or an angel from heaven should preach a gospel other than the one we preached to you, let him be eternally condemned!' (Gal. 1:8)

and into His marvellous light. We've got to preach the uncomfortable truth that they're sinners and that Christ alone can save them.

If Jesus Christ weren't the answer to man's deepest need, I would be the most miserable person on planet earth. Why? Because I'd have devoted my entire life to passing on a lie. If Jesus weren't the Saviour of the world, I would not only have to stop proclaiming the gospel, I would also have to find something else to do with my life. But what? It wouldn't make sense without Jesus on the cross. Nothing would fit if He weren't in the middle of the picture.

When you witness, you may start by sharing some of the exciting things that God is doing in your local church, but you must eventually get to the point. You won't win people by talking about the church but by preaching the gospel. The enemy will try his hardest to prevent you from sharing about Jesus. He'll pull the conversation in any other direction he can. You must firmly but lovingly bring it back. Christ must be the centre of your attention. Only He can transform the lives of sinful people and alter the destinies of nations. By proclaiming Him, you do the greatest service to the world.

▓ To do

Spend time thinking about how you would actually explain the gospel to someone. Make a note of the main points you would make. You may want to write it out in full and try it out on one of your Christian friends. Ask them for their comments.

When you are satisfied with your presentation, memorise it and be ready to use it when an opportunity arises.

➤ Write down in a notebook a brief description of different kinds of evangelism: Presence Evangelism, Evangelism through Dialogue, Social Programmes, Preaching the Gospel, etc.

➤ How will people's lives be changed by each of these methods?

➤ Why is it that preaching the gospel is more effective? 'I am not ashamed of the gospel, because it is the power of God for the salvation of everyone who believes' (Rom. 1:16a).

Is not their need urgent? If it is, does that not make evangelism a matter of urgency for us? If you knew that a man was asleep in a blazing building, you would think it a matter of urgency to try and get to him, and wake him up and bring him out. The world is full of people who are unaware that they stand under the wrath of God; is it not similarly a matter of urgency that we should go to them, and try to arouse them, and show them the way of escape?
J. I. Packer

Repent and believe

'The time has come,' he said. 'The kingdom of God is near. Repent and believe the good news!' (Mark 1:15)

God's Kingdom must have a King, and that person is the Lord Jesus Christ. When He came, He brought the Kingdom with Him. When we became Christians, we exchanged our temporary citizenship on earth for a permanent one in heaven and accepted Jesus' rule in our lives. We now prove our new citizenship by allowing Him to reign supreme over everything that we do.

Jesus preached that the Kingdom was near. Christians understand that the coming of the Kingdom is not merely a past event. It has present and future significance too. Jesus taught us to pray, 'your kingdom come' (Matt. 6:10a). He wanted people to see ever-increasing evidence of His rule on earth. But the Kingdom will not be fully established until Jesus returns in glory and claims it as His own (Rev. 11:15b). We therefore live in the tension between the 'already' and the 'not yet'. Our present-day task is to proclaim the Kingdom and extend the reign of Jesus among the nations.

Our message is not a casual, 'consider and accept' but the command, 'repent and believe'. We aren't here to 'get decisions' but to 'make disciples'. So unbelievers mustn't be allowed to

▩ To question

Which of the following reflects a Christ-centred gospel?

- Come to church and Jesus will meet your needs.
- Follow Jesus and learn how to raise your children.
- Lonely? Come to Jesus and you'll never be lonely again.
- Jesus died for you, He can forgive your sin and give you the gift of eternal life.

▩ To meditate on

The Kingdom of God is here.
'I am sending you to them to open their eyes and turn them from darkness to light, and from the power of Satan to God, so that they may receive forgiveness of sins and a place among those who are sanctified by faith in me' (Acts 26:17b,18).
'I preached that they should repent and turn to God and prove their repentance by their deeds' (Acts 26:20b).

think that they can drift effortlessly into the Kingdom. Unless there's genuine conviction of sin and whole-hearted repentance, there can be no salvation.

To repent means to turn round 180°. An unbeliever acknowledges that he has offended a holy God. He humbles himself, confesses his sin and allows Jesus to become the Lord of his life. He completely abandons his former independence and now lives solely for the King.

Repentance is for Christians too. When we're convicted about a sin, we don't try to compromise the truth. We repent. Then to prove that our repentance is genuine, we immediately change our behaviour.

Without belief, repentance doesn't mean a lot. An unbeliever may feel sorry for his sin but try to gain salvation through self-denial and good deeds. Even Christians fall into this trap. They attempt to please God by rigorously following all sorts of self-imposed rules. But they never feel that they're doing enough to earn His approval. When we believe that Christ has satisfied the law on our behalf, we are both saved and justified before God. Jesus' perfect obedience has made us completely righteous.

▓ To research

Using a concordance look up references to the word 'repent/repentance' in the New Testament.

What is the significance of repentance when presenting the gospel?

▓ Food for thought

➤ Read through Luke 15:11–32, the Parable of the Lost Son.

➤ In a notebook rewrite the story in a modern setting with a view to using it to explain repentance to a non-believer.

Repentance is not arbitrary. It is not left to our choice whether or not we will repent, but it is an indispensable command. God has enacted a law in the High Court of heaven that no sinner shall be saved except the repenting sinner, and he will not break his own law.
Thomas Watson

Biblical strategy

'As you go, preach this message: "The kingdom of heaven is near." Heal the sick, raise the dead, cleanse those who have leprosy, drive out demons. Freely you have received, freely give' (Matt. 10:7,8).

M ost believers know that they are called to tell others about Christ. What they often don't realise is that God wants them to proclaim His gospel with signs as well as words. That was Jesus' practice. Luke wrote about all that Jesus 'began to do and to teach' (Acts 1:1b). He set the precedent and expected His disciples to follow His example. What He 'began' they knew they had to continue.

He sent out the Twelve with the command to 'preach the kingdom of God and to heal the sick' (Luke 9:2b), which is exactly what they did. The seventy-two were given the same commission (Luke 10:9), which they also fulfilled. When Philip went to Samaria, he proclaimed Christ and performed miraculous signs (Acts 8:6). While Paul was preaching in Lystra, he healed a crippled man (Acts 14:8–10), and at Philippi he cast an evil spirit out of a fortune teller (Acts 16:16–18).

Jesus didn't say, 'Once the early church is established, the signs will disappear,' neither did He say, 'Miracles should be done only by eminent Christian leaders.' What He actually said was this: 'Preach the good news to all creation ... And these signs will accompany

▓ To consider

Have you ever prayed for the healing of a non-believer?

Think about specific times when a friend or acquaintance has been unwell, and consider what the impact would have been if you had prayed for them and they were healed.

Ask God to help you not to miss opportunities for praying for those around you.

▓ To meditate on

Our strategy should be to say *and* do. 'I will not venture to speak of anything except what Christ has accomplished through me in leading the Gentiles to obey God by what I have said and done — by the power of signs and miracles, through the power of the Spirit' (Rom. 15:18,19a).

those who believe' (Mark 16:15b,17a). He wants every believer to preach about the Kingdom and do the works of the Kingdom. The two cannot be separated.

A member of the church in Bangkok brought his friend to a Christmas evangelistic meeting. The visitor, a man of forty, was paralysed. A blood vessel had burst during one of his many gambling sessions and for several years he hadn't been able to move his face or any of his limbs. He was carried to the front and I prayed for him.

He recalls, 'As Dr Kriengsak laid his hands on me, I felt heat go right through my body. I began to move my hands and then my feet, and stood upright for the first time in many years. I walked around the auditorium, tears of joy running down my face ... I knew it was a miracle, and Jesus Christ was the one who had done it.' The man was saved and later led his wife and children to the Lord.

One miracle speaks 1000 words. If we're going to evangelise the world effectively, we must adopt a biblical strategy and make room for the supernatural. We must continue what Jesus has begun.

▓ Food for thought

➤ Read through Acts 8, 14, 16 and 18.

➤ In a notebook write down how many instances there are of supernatural happenings in these chapters.

➤ What impact did this have on those around?

➤ Why do signs and wonders make the preaching of the Word more effective?

▓ To do

Ask someone you know who has a healing ministry to pray with you about reaching out in this whole area of the supernatural.

Ask them if you could join them when an opportunity arises to pray for someone.

Do you want the world to see that Christianity is radically different from any other religion? Then don't stop at preaching a salvation message, do the works of the Kingdom as well. When God demonstrates His power in signs and wonders, unbelievers everywhere will marvel at what our God can and does do in the world He loves.
Mike Sprenger

Receive power, then go

On one occasion, while he was eating with them, he gave them this command: 'Do not leave Jerusalem, but wait for the gift my Father promised, which you have heard me speak about. For John baptised with water, but in a few days you will be baptised with the Holy Spirit' (Acts 1:4,5).

On occasions I've made the mistake of trying to rationalise someone into the Kingdom. It never works. Only the Holy Spirit can convict of sin and convince unbelievers that Jesus is the Christ. God doesn't want us to evangelise in our own strength, but to rely totally on Him.

Jesus was anointed for ministry. The Holy Spirit came on Him at His baptism and gave Him the authority to preach and heal. That's why there's so much emphasis in the book of Acts on the need to be filled with the Spirit. The early believers realised that if they were going to be effective for God, they had to receive His power before they went out.

Many believers look at the tremendous needs in the world and bewail their lack of spiritual power. Its secret lies in the Holy Spirit. God wants to give each of us our own 'Pentecost' experience — which is not to be confused with the need continually to be filled with the Spirit. To do the works of Christ, we must have His anointing and live each day 'according to the Spirit' (Rom. 8:4b).

Immediately the disciples had received the Spirit, they began preaching the gospel. There was no delay. They were gripped by a sense of

▓ To consider

Jesus said of Himself, 'The Spirit of the Lord is on me, because he has anointed me to preach good news to the poor,' etc. (Luke 4:18).

How much more do we need the anointing of the Spirit if we are to do all that Jesus has commanded us!

▓ To meditate on

The Holy Spirit gives us power.
'"Not by might nor by power, but by my Spirit," says the LORD Almighty' (Zech. 4:6b).
'But you will receive power when the Holy Spirit comes on you; and you will be my witnesses in Jerusalem, and in all Judea and Samaria, and to the ends of the earth' (Acts 1:8).
'Be filled with the Spirit' (Eph. 5:18b).

urgency. Jesus had given them the commission to preach the gospel to all creation and they had to get on with it. He'd told them, 'Do you not say, "Four months and then the harvest"? I tell you, open your eyes and look at the fields! They are ripe for harvest' (John 4:35).

Many Christians go around with their spiritual eyes half-closed. 'There's plenty of time,' they say casually. 'We've got to build the church first.' When they witness to unbelievers they have a 'take it or leave it' kind of attitude. 'If you're not ready to believe yet, you can come back later,' they say, and give the strong impression that there will be countless opportunities to accept Christ in the future.

Certainly we don't want to encourage quick, superficial decisions, but we must be urgent. The Bible doesn't say, 'Tomorrow is the time of God's favour, tomorrow is the day of salvation.' It's 'now' (2 Cor. 6:2b). 'The time has come,' said Jesus (Mark 1:15a) and immediately called people to repent and believe the good news.

'Open your eyes,' He says to us today. 'See the desperate need in the world. The fields are ripe for harvest. Go and reap. Seize every opportunity for the Kingdom of God.'

▓ To reflect

It may be that you have never been filled with the Spirit or that you have let your spiritual reservoir run on empty.

Ask the Lord to fill you with His Spirit now. You may need to ask someone else to pray for you and to give you an explanation of the Baptism of the Spirit.

▓ Food for thought

➢ Using a concordance look up references to the Spirit in the Old Testament and in particular the phrase 'The Spirit of the Lord came upon ... '

➢ Contrast our New Testament experience of being continually filled with the Spirit with the experience of these people in the Old Testament.

➢ Consider how much more we can achieve with the Holy Spirit permanently with us.

The Spirit equips us to serve God by imparting his gifts, directing our ministry and anointing us with power. Our horizons as far as God's service is concerned ought not to be measured therefore by our limited human capacities but by the abundant measure of the Spirit's provision.
Bruce Milne

Win the world

'You will be my
witnesses in Jerusalem,
and in all Judea and
Samaria, and to the
ends of the earth'
(Acts 1:8b).

W hat's our greatest task? To be Jesus'
witnesses 'to the ends of the earth' (Acts
1:8b). That's our scope: the whole world. If
we're focused on anything less, we're being
unbiblical.

The early believers obeyed the command.
They didn't all stay in Jerusalem and
concentrate on building the church there. They
preached the gospel throughout Judea and
Samaria (Acts 8:1b,4), Asia — or Turkey (Acts
19:10), Macedonia and Achaia — or Greece,
and beyond (1 Thess. 1:8). Within twenty years
they had touched the known world of their day.

Many Christians don't think on a global
scale. 'We've got enough problems in the local
church,' they say. 'When we've got those sorted
out, perhaps we'll change our emphasis.' But
God hasn't called us to focus on our little
corner for the time being and to embrace a
bigger vision later. If we do that we will become
frustrated with the local work which will never
seem to hang together. It's only as we look
beyond ourselves and adopt God's greater plan
that the smaller jigsaw pieces will begin to fit.

Both Old and New Testaments emphasise
God's world-consciousness. If Abraham had

▓ To consider

Ask yourself, 'How can I be a part of a
global vision'?

List ways in which you can be involved
now, e.g. prayer, financial support, etc.

Ask the Lord to show you what He
wants you to do for Him.

▓ To meditate on

Our mission is to the whole world.
'For God so loved the world that he
gave his one and only Son, that
whoever believes in him shall not perish
but have eternal life' (John 3:16).
'He is the atoning sacrifice for our sins,
and not only for ours but also for the
sins of the whole world' (1 John 2:2).